NEVER MARRY
A WRITER

Tolu' A. Akinyemi

Editing and Cover Design
Rue Collinge (The Word Tinker)

Published by 'The Roaring Lion Newcastle'
ISBN: 978-1-913636-08-1

Email:
tolu@toluakinyemi.com
author@tolutoludo.com

Website:
www.toluakinyemi.com
www.tolutoludo.com

Dedication

To my shining lights Isaac and Abigail Akinyemi, I love you more than words can convey.

CONTENTS

Acknowledgements

What a great poetcidence! Publishing two poetry collections, *Black ≠ Inferior* and *Never Marry a Writer*, on the same day gives me a feeling of immense gratitude. First to God Almighty, then to my ever-supportive family.

To "Olabisi," thanks for listening to my poems in their raw state and proffering candid advice. Thanks for always believing in my talent. A big thank you to Isaac and Abigail, for the support and encouragement at all times. I love you both now and always.

Family has been very pivotal in my literary attainment, and I want to say an immense thank you to my parents, "Gabriel and Temidayo Akinyemi," for your support through the years. I'm super grateful.

A booktiful hug to my siblings: Olushola, Oluseyi and Iretioluwa.

Sincere thanks to Dr. Temi O'Sola, my Geordie friend, for believing in the project and that the title is fitting for this collection.

Thanks to Rue Collinge for leaving a great first impression and delivering a total package. And a big thank you to the hungrybookstore for a final proofread of this collection.

A massive thank you to thinkwritten.com for inspiring a whole poetry collection out of nowhere. So booktiful that!

A final thanks to everyone who has supported me on this journey that keeps unravelling so many booktiful experiences.

POEMS

*Through the darkness, let these words
be engraved on your skin like a tattoo.*

*These words are a burden to my soul, so heavy—
this pregnancy, light as a breeze, like the one before it.*

*Dear Winner, unwrap the gift in these poems
to unleash your creative force like a giant.*

*Dear Reader, you're not an obscure piece of art,
you're not a waste of space. Say it like you*

matter.

PART I.

WRITING PEOPLE

Never Marry a Writer I

Mother's ghost will not rest in peace.
Her journals are digging up mysteries
more vivid than a reality TV show.

Her pen bleeds woes and grim hollows.
Each page wears a new kind of sad.

Father's heroic status has been eroded
like flooded land.
They say he's now the villain.

The gods have rejected the sacrifice,

painted in blood.
The red roses grieved with her. Last night,
they tumbled out of their vase and withered,
                like Mother.

Mother's words struck hard—the last laugh.

Maybe

The man in the white collar with oversized priestly garments
walked away from his marriage after thirty years.

Maybe he had a reason
that would make grown men cry their hearts out,
overwhelm young girls with the burden of marriage.

There are three sides to every story:
truth, half-baked truths and exaggerated lies.

The young man who tasted adulthood last night,
swept away by the tide of youthful exuberance,
has left home for the wild.

He said he wanted to hustle,
join the legion of superstars.

Maybe he had a reason
to be so out of control.

Stranger Conversations

I thought we had something going on—
an unholy affair, incubated in a heart
clouded with love.

The little hut that housed our blooming friendship
was swept away in the sandstorm.

My body spoke in hues and unfamiliar tongues.
I thought our chemistry was deeper
than a work of fiction.

These words wear the colour of sorrow.

Entangled

She said they were in the dark alley of sin.
On the red table of bedlam, his willpower
crumbled like a pack of cards.

Her dreary laughter ached his grieving heart,
this miserable marriage a deep gulley
which sunk him to his lowest ebb.

She was a broken piece. Lost
in the sea of flailing emotions
and a web of entanglements.

An open relationship is a bold sign of danger.
Every sound escaping from the other room
fingered his brain—felt like an intense moan.

An August visitor, whose recipe was therapy
and a cushion of love. He crushed his will to live,
smashed the red table into pieces.

August was a sour honey
that reduced her happiness count.

First Car

Our Volkswagen Beetle had finesse
and a great personality:
an eligible bachelor to the many spinsters lurking.

My first Honda is a forgotten child.
I won't fight dirty for a cheating ex.

Our Volkswagen Beetle would outshine the beetles.
It was a work of art, fit for any royal museum.

My first Honda is dead and buried.
It was laid to rest in its prime,
before it could become an albatross.

Walking in the Clouds

She was clouded in mystery. We spoke in codes
and foreign tongues only writers can unlock.

She was a queen. My heart ached
with every tear of her fragile heart.

She was untainted, a blooming rose—
her heart's yearning tugged at my soul.
We walked in the dark clouds,
                    crisscrossing,
until we became Snow White.

Our mouths hummed uncooked words
which left a bitter taste—tomorrow's bright rays,
vivid as a shining light.

The one who held the keys to her heart is in the playground
with a legion of spinsters. Say *indecisive*.

How can we break free from these shackles in the name of
love?

Let love open your eyes.

Never Marry a Writer II

Her conscience was buried in the sand,
but his words were fire to paper.

He was a writer and fighter—a word-bird
whose pen was a shooting arrow.
She was the vitriol queen
whose piercing mouth brought down seven great kings.

Their home is a den of nested words,
flying arrows and shooting pens.

Homecoming

Twenty years later, we came home to secrets
like presents forgotten under the Christmas tree.

Deep secrets unearthed—torpedoes
for his rising anger. *The one you called Father
is not your father and I can't tell who your father is.
My womb was home to many watery fluids.*

She said she was in love, but the wounds
from her heartbreaking past were a joy-killer.
The secrets were served bite-sized,
as the wind of sorrow blew.

Goodbyes

She took our love away and left me gasping for air.
This foul odour has the stench of death.

Her memory is a looming figure who leaves me
spellbound.

Our goodbyes were an obsequy of buried love.
Our eyes poured rain, lips drenched in saltwater.

Yesterday, in the garden of my heart,
I laid wreathes in despair of a better ending.

Entangled II

He would weather this bad marriage forever.
The venom of abuse has no expiry date.
Those words haunted his spirit—
til death do us part.

Her words were piercing, her mouth blowing an ill wind
in a bubble of fury.

His wedding vows gave him panic attacks,
shackles like a heavy chain.
They said she was the will of God, but his inner voice
tugged: *God is not the author of confusion.*

Their public displays of affection were picture-perfect,
but the torrents of abuse were served fresh as hot barbecue.

An evil entanglement which only ended
the day he was lowered six feet below the ground.

Never Marry a Writer III

Her ink was a spider sting
to all the brutal blows
she endured in the pit of abuse.

He trapped her in a veil of guilt.
He was a perfect muse.

Her words fell like a cross
on his shoulders. Words on paper
rang hollow, like haunting shadows.

His eyes poured an ocean,
his heartfelt cry a stirring bellow.

Cover me. Cover my naked butt this last time, he said.
This will be the last scar on your face.

Misfits

I

The measuring tape on my bulging belly is out of depth.

Wearing the tag of a weirdo in the midst of misfits
rocks my musical harmonies. My mind is a graveyard for
buried thoughts:
words and ideologies that spark an inferno.

I have found a home in the confinement of silence.

II

They said she was a lift that read *out of order*.
Her free spirit was a dog
broken free from the leash,

                              untamed.

Doctor, doctor

Anguish is a mannerless child.

A sickly woman lowers her guard, as she endures
the intensity of pain occasioned by her illness.

I could tell you were of God, immersed in anointing—
only without mercy.

Even the pope would remove the robe of pontification
and show some compassion.

Her blood is not a cross on your neck,
for she survived the ordeal.

Your words will forever remain a haunting shadow.
Take her home, she has no place here.

Grandma's Red Soup

Grandma's red soup had me on red alert.
Her recipe always triggered raging hormones.
My lips quivered and my tongue drowned
in an ocean, to calm the raging firestorm.

Grandma's red soup tasted like burning wood.
My nostrils dripped like a leaky hose.

Grandma's red soup was a thunderstorm.
Every sting on my tastebuds
sent shockwaves to my sleepy brain.

People You Have Known

They were humans first before they became dust.
Our tears filled water drums. Our nights were haunted
by fantasies of the dead.

The people you have known were fathers,
mothers, nanas, lovers. Say their names.
Hold their extinguished light aflame.

This body is a sanctuary, a home
with no permanent right of abode. These voices you heard
have disappeared into the night.
We wear grief on our sleeves.

The people you have known are kept in our minds'
museum.
Their smiles, memories, light—
now a fading memory.

These people, their spirits—
a reminder that some day
our names will be held on lips as a remembrance song.

Closure

Imperfect people hunt for perfect partners
like the villain hunting for the hero in Mission Impossible.

This is no heroic feat.
They said, *She is not the one for you*
but the one they thought a perfect choice
had more than a tonne of garbage.

She said, *I'm on the lookout for Mister Perfect*
but her bubble of anger was a punctured balloon,
damaged beyond repair.

Last week,
we laid our imperfections bare on the dinner table,
found closure and gave it another go.

PART II.

WRITING THE WRITER

Never Marry a Writer IV

Never marry a writer if your mouth is a running tap
overflowing with expletives. A writer's ink will flow
ceaselessly, like a leaking pipe.

Never marry a writer if you would like
to commit blue murder. The plot will be thicker
than a jar of honey.

Never marry a writer if you are a prisoner of emotions.
The shackles will be broken after the first chapter.

Never marry a writer if your temper is a high-tension
wire. The revelations will be more shocking
than a Daily Mail screamer.

Never marry a writer if you're prone to unending tantrums.
Your character will be nagging and miserable.

A writer is a laundry man—
he will wash your dirty laundry without a fuss.

Lion of Newcastle

In Newcastle there was a Lion King,
who wore *immigrant* like a gold crest
and found greatness in an unknown land.

Was he a Jungle King
or a man with a cacophony of voices?

Was his hair snow white, with the mind of a sage,
or the epitome of youthful vigour?

The clouds of hate gathered in torrents
as his fame was rising like yeast and swelling—
Ijebu Garri.

His god-sent angel was a bread loaf
forgotten in water.

The well of bitterness is a bottomless pit.

Dear God

I missed being a literary great by a whisker.

No eraser can wipe clean that scar from my youth.
Can't you see the dark spot that wants to trip me
on the pathway to history?

Dear God, don't close heaven's gate on me.
Hearken to my heartfelt cry.
Let me in like Auntie Nkechi
who gatecrashed my wedding party without an invite.

Don't send me headlong into that burning furnace.
I have lived under Buhari's meaningless change,
harsher than Satan's hell.

Squeeze me in like the report card that read
Promoted on trial to Year 11.

Dear God, admit me to paradise
like that sinner on the cross.
Don't let the weight of my sin
block my pathway to eternal bliss.

Ghost Writer

My pen was a burning bush, which became words on marble.

My heart brewed words like a chilled lager served on Sunday.

The convergence of ideas has turned my mind into a goldmine.

Turn the heat down! Those words sting like darts

they said.

Anointed

The hair stylist with visionary eyes
can no longer be found. He says:
You will be a Pastor. The white crust in my dark hair
is a sign, like the stars illuminating the dark sky.

I visit the salon again
and he says it once more:
You will be a pastor. I say, *Your words
are unchanged from the last time*. Twice
has he spoken; the words sink in slowly.

I have moved houses, counties, and cities.
I have had numerous stylists—weed smokers
with charcoaled lips whose mouth stench
stung the air like burning grass.

I'm on the lookout for my visionary hairstylist,
to ask God for mercy as my bibles are gathering dust.

I want to tell him that I have found my way back home,
to my Catholic roots—that I can't be a father,
as I am already a father of many nations.

A decade now. I'm desperate to see my hairstylist again.
To hear his soothing words. To tell him the closest scent
of being a pastor I have had was being labelled
Pastor's boy, before I found my way back home.

Geordie Manifesto

Another black MP in Newcastle, BBC Radio Newcastle
reveals for the umpteenth time. Not Labour, Conservative,
or the Liberal Democrats. Just a unicorn springing out of
the woods.
They say, *He's a Geordie lad—one of us*.

My Geordie manifesto bridges the divide of hate.
I wear this black suit like an oversized uniform.

My accent is a spoiler alert. *Not one of us*,
a voice bellows. My high walls crumble
like my manifesto, squeezed in sweaty palms.

Never say *originally from Nigeria*. My origin is wrapped
in egg shells—cracked like a mysterious puzzle
when the clouds of crime hang on my neck.

The icy words are only whispered behind
                    closed doors.

My anger, boiling like water, is about to stain
this watershed moment.

Screaming *Piss off!* I fling the sheet away.

A dream.
My Geordie manifesto is the stuff of dreams.

7 Days, 7 Lines

The radiant afternoon sun on Sunday has lost its aura.

Monday's cloak of busyness has been overshadowed by indolence.

The calorie counter dreads Tuesday and my busting waistline.

Wednesday is a slow burner. My heart beats faster than the clock chimes.

Thursday has lost its bubbling character, and the true plot.

Ghost towns and empty streets—the colour of Friday.

How do you write a schedule for Saturday?
Formulate strategies to survive a raging pandemic.

Lessons from School

School was painted as EUREKA!
      The gateway to paradise.

Physics brought my brain to a logjam
like a car stuck in rush-hour traffic.

I won't shed tears for not embracing the darkness of
ignorance.
I'm a free spirit, freethinker, with a mind whiter than
snow—

Life is a school of hard knocks, grind and hustle.
I'm a blooming oasis in the school of life.

Lessons from maths class gave me a new name:
Zombie.
My brain knew how to calculate money
before it could solve Pythagoras' theory.

These days I no longer think of calculus,
algebra and arithmetic formulas.
At night,
I dream of shrinking debit and imaginary credit,
and my mounting bills, higher than Idanre Hills,
become a plain valley.

I have learnt more lessons from the school of life
than any citadel of learning could teach.

Word Bandit

Copyright law—the sword of Damocles,
hanging on plagiarists. Many revered writers
have been caught in the web of plagiarism.

They said they were brimming with ideas
but their works were coloured with labels—
photocopy and *copy-copy*.

The word bandit is on the loose.
He has been declared WANTED for the umpteenth time
after he was let off the hook last week,

for pilfering plots and words.

The writer who could do no wrong
is on a downward spiral,
his fame

a
      fizzling
           candle.

Radio 6

The voice on the radio bellows
NEVER LOOK BACK!
with a voice like still water.

The last time I took a backward route,
my dreams became ice and the ice melted
into an ocean that swept them away.

Six months later, the waves washed my scattered
dreams to the seashore. I picked them up,
knitted together
                    a tattered dress.

Paranoia

These haunting shadows drive me to the woods.
This gale of evil is a running stream.
The colour of my nights is wet and lonely.

These harrowing voices are fierce, recurring.
They have built a hamlet with no lights
in a condensed part of my brain.

This stormy wave is a force of nature,
pulling my soul in every direction like an ocean,
overflowing the shore. These flailing dreams
make me edgy. My paranoia seems eternal.

Prayer

Take me to Jupiter and bury me
in the serenity of untainted bliss.
The earth is dark and grim.
How can we escape from this crystallised madness?

Transport me to Jupiter where I can live forever
in isolation. The earth has been deflowered,
soured with the sting of death.

Ferry me to a land of air and water, of peace,
devoid of the insanity that pervades the earth.

Sleepless Nights

I stare into the night with open eyes.
The window of my heart is a revolving door.

I'm looking for love in strange places.
My ex said the key to her heart was left in my suit pocket,
the one I wore over a decade ago.

My night is an action movie.
I wake up panting at the multitudes
seeking to extinguish my shining light.

Last night, I had a fight
with three faceless demons

to whom I gave immense grief and I won. Tonight,
I took communion with my eyes closed.

The blood of Jesus is a light on my lips
to redeem me from the sleepless grave.

Dusty Musical Instruments

My writing pad does not know the meaning of rusty—
it is immaculate, the colour of white gold.
My words fade into oblivion before I can string a sentence.
My wife says I'm losing my mind.

My brain is being cloned in the general market.
Last week, it was sold for the price of twenty
brains with ten years warranty and no returns offered.

My musical instruments wear dust

over their crust of white gold.

Gardening

There are days my mind feels gravelly
like an uncultivated garden. I dart around the house
looking for lost words to prey on.

I'm a towering figure with a head—
never say *figurehead*. My life's clock is gaining speed
quicker than I can fathom.

Yesterday, I was a little boy with no worries.
Today, I have a black bin of worries
gathering dust in the garden.

My former best friend has deserted me
because I didn't cry for his loss. How do I tell him
I have lost so much without shedding
more than a teardrop and a stone?

I dodged the bullet of a midlife crisis.
Every seer to peep into the mirror of my life saw greatness.
I'm still waiting for my big break.

A million books sold and mentoring young people
around Planet Earth—to soar without wavering.
I won't be caught out with the inanities and vanities of the
world.

My dreams might have crystallised
but my friends wish me well without buying my books.
They chorus, *You're the next Wole Soyinka,*
our own Shakespeare!

Their mouths are wet, but my lips are dry
from the emptiness of their words.

I detest these friends, only appearing from the woods
when in need of favours.
They say, *We have been following you for eternity!*

That line seems too recurring to be a fluke.
Woods. Secret followers. Favour–hungry friends.
Those words sum up my luck.

They vanish into thin air, until they appear from the clouds
like strange lightning when in need.

I won't be caught ranting or cussing over botched
relationships
and lost friends.
In the deepest part of my heart is a multitude.
The unread books on my shelf demand every second.
My eyes waltz through the pages
and the flipping of the pages sends the books

into a delirious spin, screaming, *He's back!*
Our love is back.

Sound of Silence

The sound of silence is an awakening light.
The stillness of my heart stirs my soul
into convulsions. Say *seventh wonder of the world*.

The sound of silence is a communion
with the realm where no mortal lives.
Think stillness of graveyards and buried dreams.

The sound of silence is a burning coal
that stirs the fire in my belly.
Rummaging for words like a cow in dung.

Silence is a temple. Haunting voices are a blur.
Cocoon me in the wings of silence,
where my nerves are calm as the sea.

Defying Gravity

This body is a moving force, like lightning.

These ocean waves are like a crushing blow.
My parachute defies this force of nature.

These thunderstorms send a message of hope.
The reverberations send them into hiding.

At the intersection where the clouds of darkness
overshadow, there is a glimmer of hope,
more than just light rays.

On the Field

I slept last night with tall dreams.
The crowd chanting my name at the Harding Stand
in Stamford Bridge snuffed out hopelessness.

Every time my leg caresses the ball,
I feel like Cristiano Ronaldo in his prime.
I'm overwhelmed with blues at the thought
that my untapped talent will haunt me to the grave.

In the field of life, I'm not a wannabe.
Google search my name and you will see my footprints
rubberstamped on the memorial grounds of history.

Don't forget to write these words on my epitaph:

The best football player of all time
who shone brightly in dreams
and on communal grounds.

A Circus of Errors

Life will not always be like a book, error-free.
Don't be that bibliophile who is on the hunt for errors.
That book was so shite! 1 star, crap as hell.

The fragments of my life have been error–strewn.
Don't remember me for the magnitude of my mistakes,
the fragility that was a connotation of my humanity.

Let the tenderness of my heart be a shining light.
Let the love that beamed through these pages erase my
scars, washing me clean.
Let my imperfections ring true.

Do not condemn me with voices that bellow hatred.
Cleanse me with the oil of forgiveness
that I might be as fresh as the morning dew.

In life, I was a colossus.
In death, let my towering figure rise
with the ferocity of a lion,

        king of the jungle.

PART III.

WRITING THE WORLD

Weirder than Fiction

2020 was the year our buzz word was *Zoom*!
It was a therapy to lighten our gloom.

Our television sets mirrored earth-shaking doom!
Doom and more doom!

This plot is darker than a work of fiction.

The unpresidential fights on Twitter
were more intense than a royal rumble.

The sledgehammer of despair bangs with a thud.

If this were a work of fiction,
it would *ribbit* and end with a ferocious growl.

This was the year humans became angels
and grief found its way into happy homes
without a pass.

Junk Mail Scam

My password has been harvested by bold-faced scammers.
Experian says my email and password are being illegally
published and sold online for twenty pence.

My junk mail is a phishing net.
They spam and spam, but my immunity from scam
is stronger than fifty white blood cells.

My junk mail prose will move you to false tears
over the magnitude of imaginary funds to give away.

My junk mail is home to Nigerian princes, Russian hackers,
Bitcoin scammers and failed con artists.

Vision

Ten shortsighted men with wobbly steps, straying.
They said they were visionaries, but they crash-landed—
         a plane of shooting stars
         and a multitude of unsung heroes.

The rhetoric-spewing visionary is on the loose again.
His words have burnt more than a thousand bridges
and clipped the wings of soaring eagles.

My American dream went up in smoke last night,
buried in the pit of racial inequality
         and selective amnesia.

Our bodies bop and sway in circles—crumbled
dreams like crunchy flakes, served at sunrise.

Our days are saturated with false hope,
until the next short-sighted visionary
repeats the cycle of stone-blind sprinting.

I draw a map with the ashes, as a remembrance.

Fake News

The morning floods in like an ocean.
I bring out my sieve to funnel out the debris.

Their voices rise like an ocean wave.
With venom, they scream FAKE NEWS!

The afternoon has been dismembered
by the fiery darts in their tongues.
Every unfavourable mouthful bit hard.

The evening wears an evil cloak, unworthy.
Its feel-good vibes have been lost in translation.

The nighttime is dark and grim, like
a hollow grave. The news gives me nightmares.

The Wall

Your favourite Instagram celebrity's wall
is a recycling bin.
Our eyes are sore from the litter
of posts, showing visible cracks.

Your favourite Instagram celebrity's wall
is laced with false algorithms,
likes dwindling by the day—
a rotten harvest.

Your favourite Instagram celebrity's wall
is a forgotten slum, their only claim to fame
is in bots and secret followers—
a fallow dump.

Your favourite Instagram celebrity lives in fading
glory. He was once treasured.
Now his folly is written
in blocks on his cracking wall.

Best Laid Plans

Turmoil wore a long dress and caught me off guard.
Causing a thunderstorm—a fierce rumble in my belly.

Life hasn't gone as planned, but I'm thirty seconds away
from becoming a multimillionaire.

My mind wanders to the crown prince, his life cut short
in his prime. He had a motley of dreams,
extinguished without a sign.

The deaths at Manchester Arena—remembering
brings a coloured mist to my eyes. Life's cruel blow.
Commiserations can't numb the stinging pain

  or   fill the void.

The cup of grief is like dark coffee—
    every day dark and sour, leaving a bitter taste.
Life won't always go as planned.
    This reality, so bitter to chew.

Standing in Line

in a land infested with barbarians,
will leave you seething with rage.
The heat from the afternoon sun is a burning coal.

Driving in traffic with law-breakers
will drive you bonkers.
These drivers from hell are a menace.

Living in a land of no rules is a deal-breaker.
The government has a hangover
while the people vomit on once-untainted land.

Season Series

Your favourite season series is a dream-killer.
She wanted to rule the world in due course
but spring soon faded with dreams unseasoned.

Your favourite season series is a showstopper.
His dreams were tall and lucid
but his castles were built in dreams.

Your favourite season series is like rotten tomatoes.
The reviews on Rotten Tomatoes scream:
Shite!

Your favourite season series has made you sour
and grumpy
because you Netflix'd and Chilled while life passed you by.

Numb

I have brain freeze in sporadic spurts.
My eyes are a well of running water.
My skin feels like peeled potatoes in need of shelter.

The agony on the TV escapes into the somber living room.
I have lost count of the anguish my soul drowns in
each time we are crucified on the altar of racial injustice.

Don't ask me why I cry and grieve for my unknown tribe—
with only a bond of shared ancestors,
we have never crossed paths.

They pierced a needle through my skin
but I can't feel it move. My body is hard as wood.
I have lost all sense of feeling.

Amnesty

The terrorists who opened the doors of hell
and drank the blood of the innocent
parade our streets with bulging shoulders.

How do I write a poem
without my tears wiping the words from
                                these
                                pages?

The terrorists who maimed and slaughtered our kin
are adorned with military uniforms as a reward.

How do I explain this to generations unborn—
that these words were not written out of context?

The terrorists who cried *education stinks like a rotten egg*
have all learnt a new vocation.

How do I maroon their ignorance in a box,
wave it off as a symptom of darkness?

The terrorists who made life a living hell
have found an alibi in the big villa.

(the dog and baboon are languishing in the hottest part of
hell)

How do you deal with these bloodsucking demons?
Reintegrate them into society,
waving the amnesty flag aloft while their victims

are   scattered,

                 the spirits of the dead

hunting for vengeance.

Blood-Stained

The green-white-green flag has been stained in blood red.
Our national anthem is no longer a song of hope.
The governors have lost control of this looming anarchy:
a car with failing brakes.

Karma strikes like a raging fire.
The army chief says they are unknown soldiers.
Speak those white lies no more—

My country kills dreams, and the generation next.
The president's speech is a bad dream.
Last night, his words cut deeply
                        like a sore wound.

Boom! Boom! Boom!
The sound from these straying bullets
                        leaves an infinite mark of sorrow.

My country is drowning in a cesspit of
                corruption and state-sponsored violence.
These failed politicians at the wheels
are driving us into extermination.

Written after the Lekki massacre on 20th October 2020, where
members of the Nigerian Army opened fire at peaceful END SARS
protesters at the Lekki toll gate in Lagos, Nigeria.

Prosperity Preachers

They told me to build my castles
in the air. Here I am, grappling at ladders in the sky.
My earthly house is sparkling white,
but my heavenly mansion is a decrepit hut.

They have turned me into a money-
minting machine. *Heaven* and *salvation*
sting my soul, a reminder
that this place is not my home. ·

These prosperity preachers sold me
false hope.
Here I am, clutching at straws, praying for manna
without daily bread.

Sign of the Times

Instagram is a glorified porn site. I say a prayer
before I am lost exploring its sinful terrain.
I beg God not to rapture the world
while I'm surfing.
The signs are ominous.

My dictionary has a case in the court of public opinion
against Google, for turning it into a useless artefact.

My calculator and mobile phone are at war again.
How do I placate those enraged
by times as unpredictable as a roll of the dice?

How do I tell you that this poem
was written with my phone's notepad
without incurring the wrath of Microsoft Word
and my notebooks, cussing.

How do I write these words—
these signs of the times—
without burning a few bridges?

Ember Months

September, October, November and December have been
labelled with the insignia of untimely death. Only in
Nigeria.

Say *ember months*. The months when the gods are on a
bloodfest and we run down our annual allocation for the
blood of Jesus
before we reach October.

The paranoia of ember months sends me into overdrive.
My prayer points are longer than the Book of Revelation.
We prayed for light, roads, good governance,
and our prayers were answered with political termites.

Don't ask me why the national treasury
bears semblance to a wooden carcass.

The pastor says, *Sanitise your life against the tide of
untimely death as we enter the ember months*.
Road safety and government have released more than a
scroll book to warn of the lurking evil.

Since I left home,
I try to dream of a September
without a thought for the evil colourations
of ember months.

On Shaky Ground

An earthquake tremor sends us scampering.
The thunderstorm of fury has left invisible scars.

The foundation on sandy ground has lost legs.
Two pillars are half-standing, groaning.

This ill wind blowing in the neighbourhood
is a telltale sign of bad news.

Who will unwrap these letters from hell?

The Untouchables

The missiles of hate hit a brick
and flapping wings ducked the arrows.

The spirit of death knocked fiercely
but the will to live issued a stinging rebuttal.

The politicians who decimated the treasure chest
have *untouchable* laminated in their darkened hearts.

The soldier whose vicious slaps
set me whimpering was untouchable.

Street Signs

The first exit was the pathway to hell.
The street sign, inked in blood, marked danger.
Every bump in the road was a ringing slap to my face.

At the evil bend, the sign read:

THIS BEND HAS TAKEN FIVE THOUSAND LIVES
AND COUNTING.

I closed my eyes, sang *hallelujah*, and inhaled the dust.
I was a guest at heaven's gate before I could say my last
prayer.

Taste the Rainbow

Can you feel the brightness of the rainbow?
Its vivid colours leave bright smiles on dour faces.

Can you smell the colours of the rainbow?
Its radiant bloom livens dead spirits.

Can you hear the cries of the rainbow?
Untangle me from the web of your pride,
                    your prejudiced labels.

Can you taste the rainbow?
Love and serenity to dock in your harbour without
flinching.

Bio

Tolu' Akinyemi is an exceptional talent and out-of-the-box creative thinker; a change management agent and a leader par excellence. Tolu' is a business analyst, financial crime consultant, and a Certified Anti-Money Laundering Specialist (CAMS) with extensive experience working with leading investment banks and consultancy firms. Tolu' is also a personal development and career coach and a prolific writer with more than 10 years writing experience. He is a mentor to hundreds of young people. He worked as an Associate Mentor in St. Mary's School, Cheshunt and as an Inclusion Mentor in Barnwell School, Stevenage in the United Kingdom, helping students raise their aspirations and standards of performance and helping them cope with transitions from one educational stage to another.

A man whom many refer to as "Mr Vision," he is a trained economist from Ekiti State University (formerly known as University of Ado-Ekiti (UNAD)). He sat his Masters' Degree in Accounting and Financial Management at the University of Hertfordshire, Hatfield, United Kingdom. Tolu' was a student ambassador at the University of Hertfordshire, Hatfield, representing the University in major forums and engaging with young people during various assignments.

Tolu' Akinyemi is a home-grown talent; an alumnus of the Daystar Leadership Academy (DLA). He is passionate about people and wealth creation. He believes intensely that life is about impacting others. In his words, "To have a secure future, we must be willing to pay the price in order to earn the prize."

Tolu' has headlined, and been featured in, various Poetry Festivals, Open Slam, Poetry Slam, Spoken Word and Open Mic events in and outside the United Kingdom. He also inspires large audiences through spoken word performances. He has appeared as a keynote speaker in major forums and events, and facilitates creative writing master classes to many audiences.

Tolu' Akinyemi was born in Ado-Ekiti, Nigeria and lives in the United Kingdom. Tolu' is an ardent supporter of the Chelsea Football Club in London.

You can connect with Tolu' on his various Social Media Accounts:

Instagram: @ToluToludo
Facebook: facebook.com/toluaakinyemi
Twitter: @ToluAkinyemi

Author's Note

Thank you for the time you have taken to read this book. I hope you enjoyed the poems in it.

If you loved the book and have a minute to spare, I would appreciate a short review on the page or site where you bought it. I greatly appreciate your help in promoting my work. Reviews from readers like you make a huge difference in helping new readers choose the book.

Thank you!
Tolu' Akinyemi

Dead Lions Don't Roar

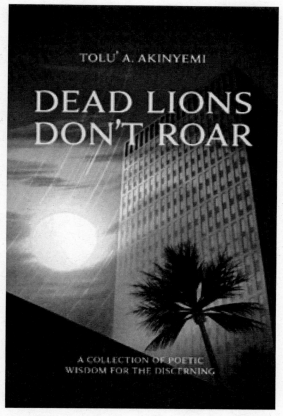

In a society where moral rectitude is increasingly becoming abeyant, Akinyemi's bounden duty is to reawaken it with verses. He, thus, functions as a philosopher-poet, a kind of factotum inculcating wisdom in different facets of life. Dead Lions Don't Roar leads us into the universe of an exact mind rousing the lethargic from indolence or prevarication, bearing in mind that the greatest achievers are those who take the bull by the horn. Taking a step can just be the open sesame to reach the stars. Enough of jeremiad! - **The Sun**

Dead Lions Don't Roar, a collection of poetic wisdom for the discerning, makes an interesting read. A paper pack, the poems are concise, easy to digest, travel friendly and express deep feelings and noble thoughts in beautiful and simple language. **-The Nation**

Akinyemi's verses are concise, straight-edge and explanatory, reminiscent of the kind of poetry often churned out by Mamman J. Vatsa, the late soldier and poet. **–yNaija**

Dead Lion's Don't Roar is a collection of inspiring and motivating modern-day verses. Addressing many issues close to home and also many taboo subjects, the poetry is reflective of today's struggles, and lights the way to a positive future. The uplifting book will appeal to all age groups and anyone going through change, building or enjoying a career, and facing day to day struggles. Many of the short verses will resonate with readers, leaving a sense of peace and wellbeing.

Dead Cats Don't Meow

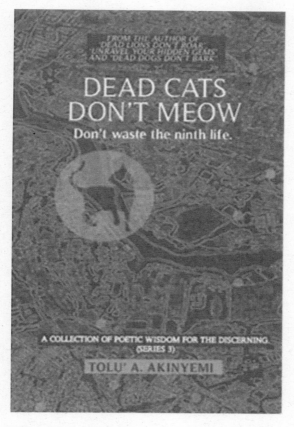

In all, this poetry collection *Dead Cats Don't Meow* generally emphasizes the theme of self-belief and taking action. It reminds me of the saying "if you think you are too little to make an impact, try staying in a room with a mosquito." **- BellaNaija.**

Overall, *Dead Cats Don't Meow* comes across as a collection of thoughtful poetry that inspires, entertains, and educates its reader. It is a great blend of themes spanning across love, inspiration, politics, entrepreneurship, marriage and life, among others. Its simplicity eludes intentionality, and the plays on words show experience.

The collection is suitable for both the literary and non-literary community and is a great work for all manner of readers. I believe, with this one, Akinyemi has achieved his goals of motivation.

- The Nation Newspaper.

Dead Cats Don't Meow urges its readers not to waste their ninth life...the author of the collection of poetic wisdom for the discerning adds his third compendium of poems to the bookshelves alongside *Dead Lions Don't Roar* and *Dead Dogs Don't Bark*. Tolu A. Akinyemi, renowned poet, author and performer, brings to us *Dead Cats Don't Meow*, a metrical masterpiece which invokes love and respect for life with every word. Each poem examines a part of life, a sensation, a reaction, or an emotion. Beautifully written...individually, the verses breathe their own beat, whilst the collection knits together perfectly to present an idyllic collection to attain innate potential. "Don't waste the ninth life! Don't miss the chance to add this rare compendium of poetic wisdom to your bookshelf today!"

Unravel Your Hidden Gems

Unravel Your Hidden Gems is like a Solomon talking to us in the 21st century. The book teaches us to value what we have, the pursuit of excellence, and, above all, steps to unravel your hidden gems, drawn from your extraordinary talents, deposited in you right from the first day the placenta was severed from the womb. A book for all seasons, no doubt, especially in Africa where aspirations sometimes do not match inspirations, it is only logical that you add it to your shopping cart. - **Guardian Arts**

Watching others ascend the totem pole of life with relative ease, some come to believe they can't fly. Times without number, they have tried, yet they have found no way to break the ice. Don't despair if you are unsettled by a losing streak.

Tolu Akinyemi, the author of *Unravel Your Hidden Gems,* believes that the hero lies in you. If only you can discover the hidden gems in you, you are on your way to excelling. How, then, do you dig deep into the labyrinth for the gems?

Unravel Your Hidden Gems is a 376-page book by a prolific UK-based Nigerian author. It is a collection of over 360 inspirational and motivational essays from a young man who feels he has a mission to rouse dampened spirits to make the much-needed push in life to regenerate abundantly.

In seven parts, the author makes a diligent search into typical problems encountered by men, capable of weighing them down, and comes up with snippets of wisdom. **- The Sun**

Unravel your Hidden Gems is a collection of inspirational and motivational essays from the heart of the acclaimed author, Tolu' A. Akinyemi. Released hot on the heels of Tolu's first book of poetry, *Dead Lions Don't Roar*, this new book is a study on Life, encouraging people to succeed at what they feel is important to their own happiness. Be it private life, business, religion, career, or relationships, each part of life is discovered. This mind-altering life manual can be read as a whole or visited in snippets for day to day inspiration. Each essay examines and highlights challenges in life and how to succeed in enjoying life with grace. A self-help study on life with a refreshing difference, the book is a totality of life's journey, reminding us we are here on a temporary basis and that it is our duty to not hide in obscurity, but to Unravel Your Hidden Gems before it is too late! Pure Inspiration!

Dead Dogs Don't Bark

Dead Dogs Don't Bark is as culturally relevant as can be, and this deserves commendation. – **Bellanaija**

In a nutshell, Dead Dogs Don't Bark is enjoyable, it is stimulating. **- Bdaily UK**

The collection takes this reader through an exhilarating journey of wits and pun. The power of words, both grand and subtle, is that it allows the reader to place himself in the scheme and feel the poems on a more visceral level. Creating concrete imageries, the poet says even before it sticks out its tongue and bares its teeth, the first thing that defeats a fainthearted in an unfamiliar threshold is the bark of a dog. It sends cold shivers running down the spine. That very bark, disarming as it is, is the dog's way of calling attention: I am here! - **Guardian Arts**

Dead Dogs Don't Bark is the second poetry collection from the acclaimed author Tolu' A. Akinyemi. With a similar tone and style *to Dead Lions Don't Roar* (Tolu's first poetry collection) this follow-up masterpiece is nothing short of pure motivation. The poems cover a range of topics that many in life are aware of, that the Author himself has experienced and that we all, whatever our age, need support in.

Beautifully written, the poems speak volumes to all age groups as they feature finding your inner talent and celebrating your individuality and distinct voice. The poetry collection has didactic elements for evaporating the effects of peer pressure and criminality amongst many others. Also covering mental health, relationships, career focus, and general life issues, the poetry is bittersweet, amusing, and thought-provoking, in turns.

Never Play Games With The Devil

TOLU' A. AKINYEMI

NEVER PLAY GAMES
WITH *The* DEVIL

Reflective, insightful, and ultimately inspirational, *Never Play Games with the Devil* is a collection best digested slowly and thoughtfully. It's a series of insights and admonitions about life's purposes and coping mechanisms for "...*not crashing under the weight of the world.*"
D. Donovan, Senior Reviewer, Midwest Book Review

Readers will find Akinyemi's reflections on significant life issues completely relevant, sharply logical, and deeply felt. -

The Prairies Book Review

Hear the poet as, in a succinct moment of self-adulation, he writes:

"My brain thinks faster than my words can convey. My mind works magic. Can I live this life forever?"

Divided into three sections, *Never Play Games with the Devil* showcases a poet at the height of his powers, exploring several themes in different voices.

In the first section, the poet is the charismatic preacher encouraging people to Hustle, Find their Feet and Grow. He writes about the lot of Broken Men crashing under the weight of expectations; he talks about boys like Eddie and Edmund, bullied for the shape of their heads. He humorously addresses the consequence of choices in the title poem, 'Never Play Games with the Devil.'

The second section secures him a seat as an activist. We see the poet tackle, in verse, despotic and undemocratic governments, marauding killer herdsmen, and the pastor who lost his voice. The poet mourns the hapless souls in the crossfire between society's rot and the State's insouciance.

The final poems explore the basis of human relationships. The poems here deal with love, commitment, and trust.

Never Play Games with the Devil is a didactic collection of poems on pertinent life issues. These poems draw their appeal from the poet's ability to sustain a figment of thought through the entire span of each poem.

A Booktiful Love

Poet Tolu' A. Akinyemi tackles life with a passionate, analytical, observing eye and creates admonitions which pull at emotional strings in the heart. Poetry readers who choose his free verse collection will find it equally powerful whether it's considering divorce and grief or the love language of 'A Booktiful Love'. **- D. Donovan - Senior Reviewer, Midwest Book Review.**

Readers will find Akinyemi's collection an intriguing

approach to exploration of the entirety of human experience in its various forms. This is a superb collection. - **The Prairies Book Review.**

A Booktiful Love is a collection of poems that deal with the entirety of human experience in its various forms. Didactically rich, the poems explore ideas ranging from love, relationships, and patriotism to marriage, morality, and many other concepts pertinent to daily living.

Given its variety of themes, what unifies the poems in this collection is the simplicity and ambiguousness of language which the poet employs. The poems draw their strength from their clarity and meaning.

These are poems with a purpose. Poet Tolu' A. Akinyemi didn't shy away from this fact, as he wrote in the poems "Writers" and "Write for Rights." The poet's philosophy is evident in this collection. To him, a writer is saddled with the responsibility to use his words to teach, preach, and fight for freedom.

He writes:

"Let's change the world, one writer at a time,
Write those words till the world gets it right."

Another special attribute to this collection is the poet's experimentation with words. This is clear right from the title. The poet identifies himself as a creator of words. The reader is obliged to travel into the mind of the writer in each poem, to understand how his mind works. As readers approach the end of this collection, they not only become engrossed in its didactic richness, but also will appreciate the uniqueness of the poet's style and the sense of responsibility he carries.

Inferno of Silence

INFERNO OF
SILENCE

(A COLLECTION OF SHORT STORIES)

Be a Man

Real men don't cry

Women and children first

Are you not a man ?

Men cannot be raped, you are lying

ow can she beat you?

TOLU A. AKINYEMI

Inferno of Silence is a wide-ranging collection that tackles different themes of love, life, interpersonal relationships, and social and political challenges. It's a hard-hitting, revealing collection that keeps readers engaged and thinking with each short exploration of characters who confront their prejudices, realities, and the winds of change in their lives.

Readers of literary explorations that include African cultural influence and modern-day dilemmas will find this collection engrossing. - **D. Donovan, Senior Reviewer, Midwest**

Book Review

Poignant and honest...

Akinyemi's first collection of short stories dazzles with elegant prose, genuine emotions, and Nigerian cultural lore as it plumbs both the socio-cultural issues and the depths of love, loss, grief, and personal trauma. Lovers of literary fiction will be rewarded. - **The Prairies Book Review**

The first collection of short stories by this multitalented author entwines everyday events that are articulated in excellent storytelling.

The title story "Inferno of Silence" portrays men's societal challenges and the unspoken truths and burdens that men bear, while "Black lives Matter" shows the firsthand trauma of a man facing racism as a footballer plying his trade in Europe.

Stories range from "Return Journey" where we encounter a techpreneur/ Poet/Serial Womanizer confronting consequences of his past actions, to "Blinded by Silence," where a couple united by love must face a political upheaval changing their fortune.

These are completed with stories of relationships: "Trouble in Umudike" – about family wealth and marriage; "Everybody don Kolomental" where the main character deals with mental health issues; and "In the Trap of Seers" when one's life is on auto-reverse with the death of her confidante, her mother, as she takes us through her ordeal and journey to redemption. This is a broad and very inclusive collection.

BLACK ≠INFERIOR

TOLU' A. AKINYEMI

Akinyemi employs a steady hand and heart to capturing Black lives in various nuances, from political and social arenas to personal experience: *"Equality is a forgotten child. The blood of the innocents/soil the World. Racial Injustice walks tall,/the graves of our ancestors quake in anguish/at this perpetual ignominy."*

This juxtaposition of the personal and the political makes *Black#Inferior* a particularly important read. It holds a compelling, accessible message to the Black community in the form of hard-hitting poems which offer emotional observations of the modern state of Black minds and societies around the world.

Poetry readers interested in the fusion of literary ability and social inspection will appreciate the hard-hitting blend of both in *Black#Inferior,* which is recommended reading for a wide audience, especially students of Black experience.- *D. Donovan - Senior Reviewer, Midwest Book Review.*

A celebration of black culture and experience and life in general, the collection makes for an electrifying read. - *The Prairies Book Review.*

Black ≠ Inferior is a collection of poems divided into 2 parts. The first part is a collection of thematically linked poems exploring Blackness and the myriads of issues it attracts. The second part oscillates themes— talking about consent, a query of death, a celebration of love among others. In his usual stylistic, this collection deals with weighty matters like race and colourism with simple and clear language.

In Black ≠ Inferior, we see Tolu' Akinyemi reacting in response to the world, to issues that affect Black people. Here, we see a poet shedding off his burdens through his poems; hence, the beauty of this collection is in the issues it attempts to address. In this collection, Tolu' wears a coat of many colours – he is a preacher, a prophet, a doctor and a teacher.

We see Tolu' the preacher in these lines:
'I wish you can rise through the squalor of poverty and voices that watercolour you as under-represented.
I wish you can emblaze your name in gold, and swim against every wave of hate.'

This is a collection of poems fit for the present narrative as any (Black) person who reads this collection should beam with confidence at the end. This is what the poet sets out to achieve with his oeuvre.